Dedicated to my family in the United States and Colombia, and my friends at Lindbergh-Schweitzer Elementary. Thank you all for teaching me that people with disabilities have a right to be educated, included, and loved.

   – Alex Montoya

Dedicated to my friends and family, who are always there to provide their support. And to Alex Montoya for his friendship and leadership.

   – Beto Gurmilan

Dedicated to my family, friends, and all the healthcare and essential workers who risked their lives to save others.

   – Maghan Gallagher

Alex Montoya was a new baby boy
And when he was born, his family felt joy
Colombia, South America, was where he was born
But some of the doctors felt rather torn.
He was born with ONE leg, instead of two
And where babies have arms, only short stubs grew
The official term was "triple amputee"
Missing three limbs, unlike you and me.
"We're so sorry," the doctors said
To Alex's mother at her hospital bed
"Sorry for what?!" his parents exclaimed
"We're proud that this boy will carry our name!"

When Alex came home, neighbors were curious
They looked and they stared, which made his family furious
Both of his parents and sister and brother
Told every person, one after another
So that people learned, very quickly in fact
It was ok to ask, "Why was Alex born like that?"
And his parents would patiently and calmly say:
"We're used to everyone looking a certain way…
But when Alex was born, he had a birth defect…
Missing a leg and two arms, which we didn't expect…
Life will be challenging for our beautiful son…
But we will adore him and his life will be fun!"

As a young boy, his parents were right

Life was more challenging than most kids' lives might

"But enjoy every day," his parents said

"And if people stare at you, do this instead...

Say, 'Hi, I'm Alex, will you be my friend?

And I'll answer your questions all the way to the end!'

When he turned two, Shriner's Hospitals reached out

Helping young kids is what they were about

One thing they did, which was really so cool

Was provide prosthetic limbs and help kids go to school!

A prosthetic limb is an artificial one

A leg or an arm, so they can write, jump, or run

So, Alex made the move to a brand-new land

And received two hooks to serve as his hands

The Shriners gave him a leg, made out of wood

Now he could walk like all the kids could!

Every day he practiced real hard
At home, with his family, or in the front yard
It was not easy, and he couldn't do everything
"But never give up," said his Mom, "You Can Do Anything!"

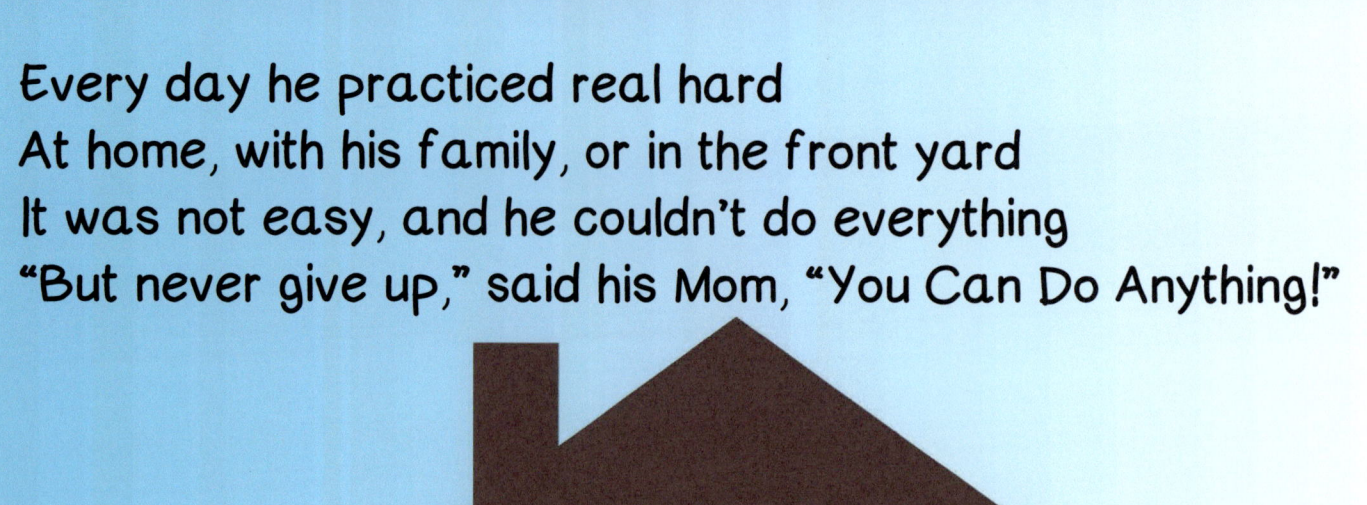

Soon it was time to try something cool

For Alex to become a student at school!

And his family said: "When your classmates ask, talk for a while

Be extra friendly and give them a smile!"

In this manner, Alex made friends
It was ok that the questions never would end

"You can do it!"

That was alright because kids wanted to know

How do your arms move with such flow?

One day Alex received a special invitation
From several friends, after he mentioned,
"I sure would love to play on those monkey bars
It sure looks fun, even if you get funky scars!"
A couple of friends said, "Well, what's the fuss?
Why don't you play on the monkey bars with us?"
Alex was really and truly amazed
He had been wanting to do this for days!

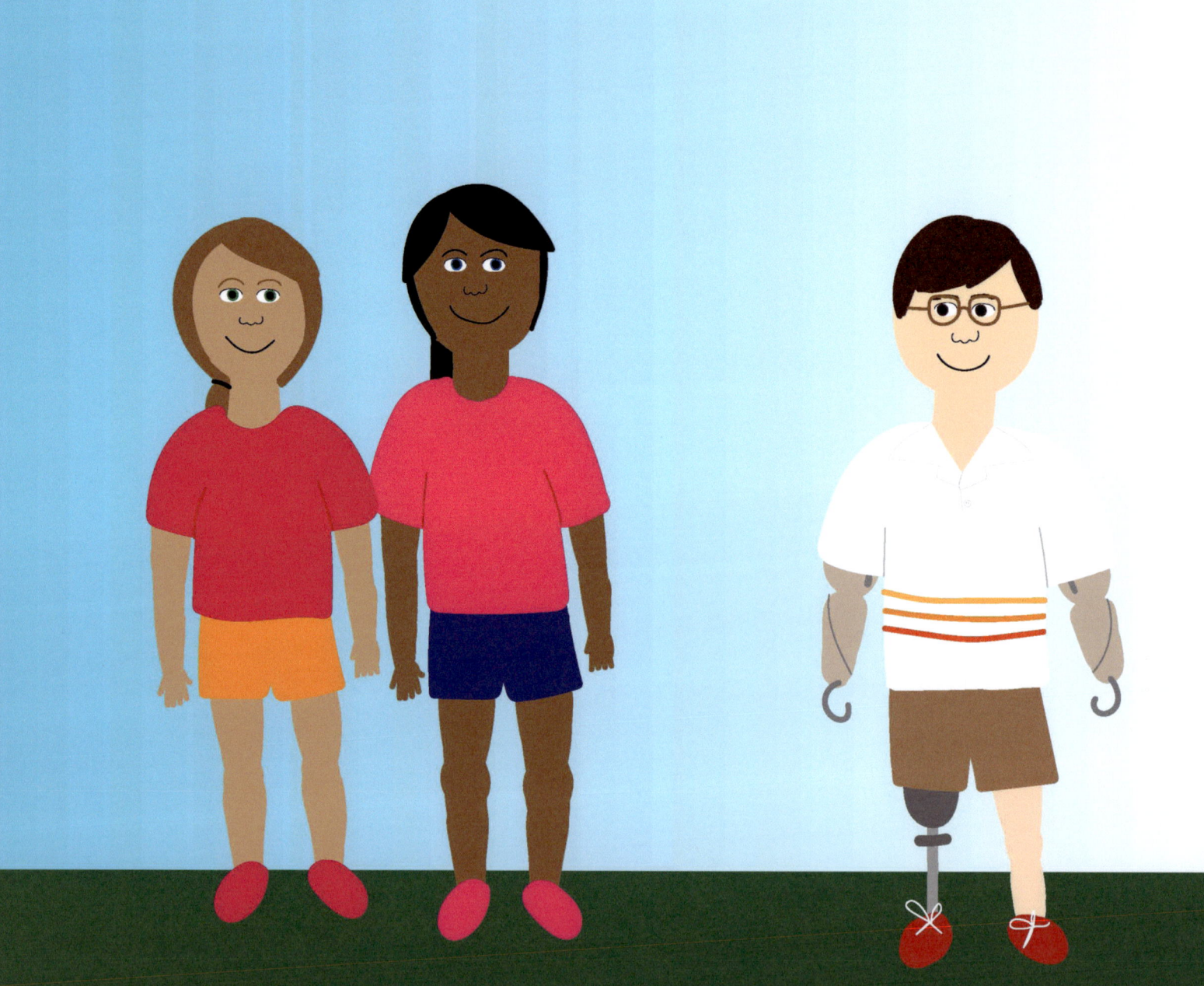

But a couple of kids had words to say:
"You climb the monkey bars? Yeah, right! No way!"
Alex was sad and then he sighed
Climb up the monkey bars? Well – he'd never tried!
Then two girls stepped forward to say
"We have an idea that may save the day
Alex, put down your backpack of books
And grab onto this ladder with both of your hooks
Then take your left leg, which is good and strong
And drag the other leg, and we can't go wrong!"

"A-LEX! A-LEX!" ALL the kids yelled
And he knew they were close, just in case he fell
So he said, "Today, my friends, we reach for the stars
I'm gonna master the monkey bars!"

Alex put his two hooks on the bars of the ladder
He knew concentration especially mattered
Then with his left leg he pushed all his weight
And dragged his right leg – this idea worked great
Up he climbed
up, up, up

And ALL the kids, even the ones who had doubted
Were all so excited, they high-fived and shouted

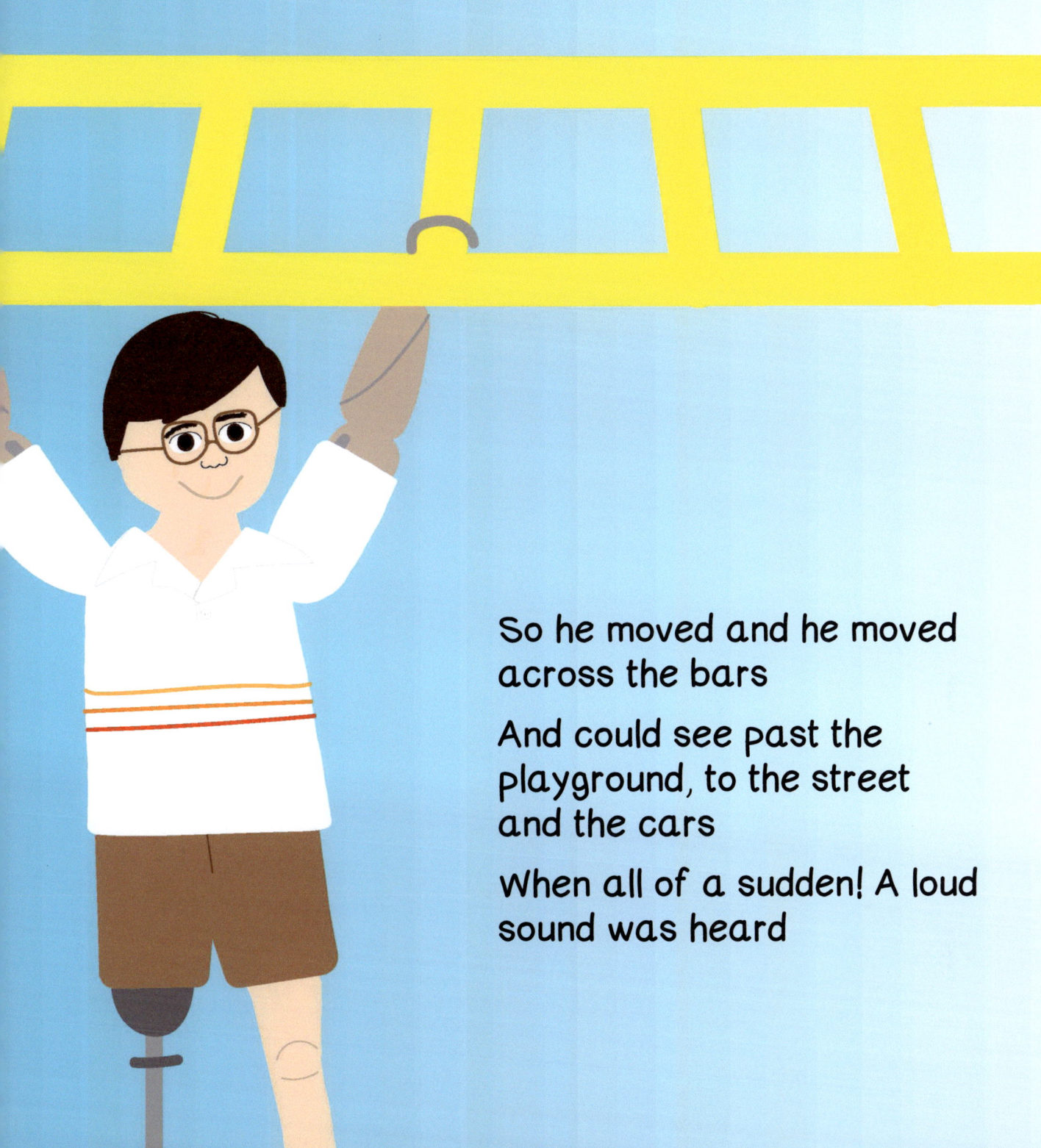

So he moved and he moved across the bars

And could see past the playground, to the street and the cars

When all of a sudden! A loud sound was heard

It wasn't a car and it wasn't a bird

The buzz was a bell, the school bell in fact

And all of the kids had to get back

To their classes and teachers and all of their friends

Just like that, recess came to an end

He thought to himself, "What do I do? What should I try?

My friends have left me hanging so high!"

He waited and waited, and a few minutes passed

When all of a sudden, he saw someone walking real fast!

"Alejandro Montoya Gonzalez!" a loud voice yelled
She used his full name, he could immediately tell
It was his teacher, oh yes, who looked up and asked

"Why aren't you with the others in class?"

And said, "Aw, I'm so sorry...
I'm just Hangin' Around!"

So when you feel down, remember this day
Where Alex's friends showed a very kind way

From that day on, he joined his friends every day
Mastering the monkey bars in every which way

Alex went on to achieve many dreams
As hard as it sounds, as hard as it seems
So, if someone with a disability is in your school or class
Just be friendly and go ahead and ask!

Remember this story, all you kids, near and far
Of the day some great friends
Helped Alex master the monkey bars.

ABOUT THE AUTHORS

ALEX MONTOYA, Author

Alex Montoya is an award-winning author and motivational speaker. His previous books are all on Amazon: *Swinging for the Fences* (2008), *The Finish Line* (2012), *See the Good* (2016), *Wolfpack* (2017), and *Living Inspired* (2018). He is a recipient of a Colombian Medal of Honor and graduate of the University of Notre Dame. Based in San Diego's East Village, he is also on the Board of Directors for the Gurmilan Foundation. This is his first children's book and you may learn more about his disability-awareness and inspirational presentations at www.alexmontoya.org.

BETO GURMILAN, Executive Editor

Beto Gurmilan is an award-winning educator, author, and speaker. He is the President of the San Ysidro School Board (San Ysidro, CA), community college instructor, and founder of the Gurmilan Foundation, which provides support and scholarships to people with disabilities. He is also the author of *From My Chair* (2016) and speaks on behalf of the Foundation to schools, businesses, and civic organizations.

MAGHAN GALLAGHER, Illustrator

Maghan Gallagher is a rising star in the illustration and design world. After a nationwide search, she was selected to illustrate this book as a senior at Guerin Catholic High School in Westfield, Indiana. A member of the National Honor Society, she is well-versed in many forms of art and also enjoys feature films.

This book was created on Amazon's Print-on-Demand platform.

Printed by Libri Plureos GmbH in Hamburg, Germany